NATIONS IN CONFLICT

COLOMBIA

by Chris Hughes

WITHDRAWN

BLACKBIRCH PRESS

An imprint of Thomson Gale, a part of The Thomson Corporation

THOMSON

★

™

GALE

Detroit • New York • San Francisco • San Diego • New Haven, Conn. • Waterville, Maine • London • Munich

Photo credits:
Cover Image: © Reuters/ CORBIS
© ALBEIRO LOPERA/Reuters/CORBIS, 17
© Alessia Pierdomenico/Reuters/CORBIS, 4
AP/Wide World photos, 42
© Bettmann/CORBIS, 15, 22
© Carl & Ann Purcell/CORBIS, 8
© Christie's Images/CORBIS, 10
© Eduardo Munoz/Reuters/CORBIS, 34
© El Espectador/CORBIS SYGMA, 27
Getty Images, 20, 24, 36, 39, 41
© Gustavo Gilabert/CORBIS SABA, 19
© Reuters/CORBIS, 6, 19 (inset), 30, 32, 43
© Rovar Willy/CORBIS, 29
Steve Zmina, 5
The Art Archive/Simon Bolivar Amphitheatre Mexico/Dagli Orti, 13

LIBRARY OF CONGRESS CATALOGING-IN-PUBLICATION DATA

Hughes, Christopher (Christopher A.), 1968-
   Colombia / by Chris Hughes.
     p. cm. — (Nations in conflict)
   Includes bibliographical references and index.
   ISBN 1-4103-0554-6 (hard cover : alk. paper)
   1. Drug traffic—Colombia—History—20th century—Juvenile literature. 2. Political violence—Colombia—History—20th century—Juvenile literature. 3. Guerrillas—Colombia—History—20th century—Juvenile literature. 4. Insurgency—Colombia—History—20th century—Juvenile literature. 5. Colombia—Politics and government—1974—Juvenile literature. I. Title. II. Series.
   F2279.H84 2005
   986.1—dc22   2005009567

CONTENTS

A Web of Conflict

By the time Alvaro Uribe was elected president of the South American nation of Colombia in 2002, he had already survived multiple assassination attempts. On the day he was installed as president, a series of bombs rocked the presidential palace and the nearby area. The bombs killed nineteen people but missed Uribe. He has survived several more murder attempts since his presidency began, as he continues to hold his very risky job.

Uribe governs one of the world's most violent and dangerous nations—a nation in which several different groups have established their own armies and claimed sections of the country as their own. In addition to long-standing rebel armies and antirebel

President Alvaro Uribe has the difficult and dangerous job of securing peace for troubled Colombia.

Caribbean
Sea

PANAMA

VENEZUELA

Pacific Ocean

● Medellín

★ Bogotá

● Cali

COLOMBIA

Equator

ECUADOR

BRAZIL

PERU

Amazon River

Colombia provides 80 percent of the world's powder cocaine. Here, a peasant displays a bag of semi-refined cocaine at a drug lab in the Colombian jungle.

armies that work outside of the government's control, Colombia has some of the strongest illegal drug organizations in the world. These drug organizations have their own armies, which have more money and better weapons than many countries have.

The conflict in Colombia is complicated. Several of these groups have at times worked with each other and at other times fought each other violently. Drug money has been linked to every major group in Colombia, including the government. The most frequent victims of the violence are Colombia's poor, who are caught in the middle of the conflicts. In 2004, Human Rights Watch declared, "Colombia leads the Western hemisphere in reported human rights and international humanitarian law violations."[1]

Colombia's most important international partner is the United States. The relationship was not always good: The U.S. Navy helped Panama break free from Colombia in 1903. Over the past century, however, Colombia and the United States have built some strong political connections. In fact, the United States has been Colombia's strongest supporter in recent years, even though it is estimated that Colombia produces 80 percent of the world's powder cocaine supply and most of the powder cocaine and heroin sold in the United States. After promising $1.3 billion to Colombia to fight drugs in 2000, the United States has continued to support Uribe in his quest to gain control and achieve peace in this troubled land.

CHAPTER ONE

Place, People, Past

South America's fourth-largest country is the only nation on the continent with coasts on both the Pacific Ocean and the Caribbean Sea. Colombia borders Venezuela, Panama, Brazil, Peru, and Ecuador, and the country has a widely varied environment. Most of western Colombia is mountainous. The Andes Mountains that run throughout western South America divide into three different ranges in Colombia. The lowlands in the east and north include dense jungles, flat grasslands, deserts, and major rivers.

Many scientists claim that Colombia has more plant and animal species for its size than any other country in the world. There are more species of birds found in Colombia, for example, than in all of Europe and North America combined. A United Nations report states that Colombia's Chocó region, along the western coast, "possesses the greatest plant biodiversity on the planet."[2]

Most Colombians are of mixed heritage, resulting from centuries of intermarriage and relations between Europeans, former African slaves, and the indigenous people who were there before the Europeans arrived. Only about 1 percent of the people are full descendants of those early

Farms stretch across the hills and valleys of the Colombian landscape. The nation is also made up of dense jungles, deserts, and major rivers.

Colombian cultures. Spanish heritage remains very strong: About 90 percent of Colombians are Roman Catholic, and Spanish is the official language.

Defeating Spain for control over Colombia in 1819, Simon Bolívar was named president of Gran Colombia.

Colombia's Early History

The Spanish first arrived in Colombia in 1499 and established their first permanent settlement in 1525. They found a land populated mostly by small, isolated communities of hunters and farmers. The largest community, the Chibcha, lived around what is today the capital of Bogotá in central Colombia. Gold, which was used as a religious item by the natives, made Colombia very attractive to Spain. The Spanish created the Viceroyalty of New Granada in 1717. It included modern Venezuela, Colombia, Panama, and Ecuador, and was headquartered at Bogotá. For most of the following century, Bogotá was one of the most important cities in the Spanish empire.

By the turn of the 19th century, many citizens of Spanish

lands in the Americas were growing restless. They were tired of being controlled from the courts of Spain, and they resented the heavy tax burdens they bore. In 1810, citizens of Bogota rose up against Spain's rule. Colombia's fight for freedom from Spain continued for nine years. Under the leadership of Simon Bolívar and Francisco de Paula Santander, Spain's forces in New Granada were finally defeated at the Battle of Boyacá in 1819. Bolívar was named president of the new nation, called Gran Colombia (Greater Colombia), with Santander as his vice president.

Bolívar and Santander

Bolívar led the fight for independence against the Spanish throughout most of northern and western South America, including Venezuela, Colombia, Ecuador, Peru, and Bolivia. Because of his popularity, Bolívar's views on government were very influential. He thought that the people of South America, who were used to a king and queen, would respond only to a government with a powerful leader at the center. Bolívar wanted an elected president who would serve for life, and he only wanted certain influential landowners to be able to vote.

Santander ran Colombia for most of the first several years of its independence, while Bolívar was fighting in Peru and Bolivia. Santander's views on government were more moderate than Bolívar's were. He wanted elections to be open to more people, and he wanted more limits on the power of the government than Bolívar did.

Over time, the differences between Bolívar and Santander came to represent the two strongest political groups in Colombia. Conservatives were those who followed Bolívar. They wanted limited voting rights, a strong

"THE LIBERATOR" SIMON BOLÍVAR

Born in 1783, in what would become Venezuela, Simon Bolívar was a child of wealthy parents. They provided him with a strong education both at home and in Spain. His upbringing caused him to resent the influence of Spain on the lives of people in the Americas. They were expected to pay high taxes, but they had limited input into major decisions that affected them. All power was held by the Spanish Court or by politicians who spent most of their time in Spain.

In 1810, Bolívar joined a junta, or "military government," in Venezuela that opposed Europe's control. That group was defeated, but Bolívar tried again in 1813. He enjoyed initial success, freeing the major cities of Merida, Caracas, and Bogotá, and earning the title El Libertador, or the "Liberator." In 1814, however, Bolívar was again defeated. He fled to Jamaica and later Haiti. There, he gathered his forces and made plans for a new attempt to free his homeland.

In 1816, Bolívar began his greatest quest. He conquered the area that is now Venezuela in 1817 and freed Colombia (including modern Panama) in 1819. Later that year, he added Ecuador to the freed lands and created the new nation of Gran Colombia, made up of those four countries. Although Bolívar named himself president of Gran Colombia, his work against the Spanish was far from done.

Spain's armies in Argentina and Chile had been defeated by local juntas and by an Argentine general named José de San Martín. By 1821, Spain controlled only Peru and Bolivia (then called Upper Peru) in South America, with the Spanish capital at Lima, Peru. As San Martín attacked Peru from the south, Bolívar attacked from Ecuador in the north. Fearing that he and

A portrait titled *The Liberator* celebrates Simon Bolívar's various defeats of Spanish forces.

Bolívar might end up fighting for control over the anti-Spanish forces, San Martín resigned in 1821, leaving Bolívar in sole command. Bolívar was named president of Peru, and by 1825 the Spanish forces in South America had been completely defeated. The next year, Upper Peru was renamed Bolivia in his honor, and the Bolivian leaders asked him to write their constitution.

Bolívar favored a strong ruler, and the constitution he wrote called for an elected president who would serve for life. His own presidency, however, was not successful. He retired in 1828, and in 1830 both Venezuela and Ecuador withdrew from Gran Colombia. Bolívar died in 1830 and is still honored throughout northern South America as the hero who brought independence.

central government, and close ties between the government and the Roman Catholic Church. Liberals were those who approved of Santander's views. They wanted wider voting rights, less central power, and more separation between church and state than the Conservatives wanted.

Political Struggles

In 1830, Gran Colombia broke apart. Venezuela and Ecuador declared themselves independent, and the remaining land became the Republic of New Granada. That name was changed to the United States of Colombia in 1863 and finally to the Republic of Colombia in 1886. Each name change came as a new government took over the nation. The Conservative and Liberal parties constantly fought for control, leading to a number of battles and government takeovers. In 1899, a full civil war broke out. Called the War of a Thousand Days, it cost more than 100,000 lives before it ended in 1902.

The following year, the United States became directly involved in Colombia's affairs. The United States was interested in building a canal through the narrow region in northwest Colombia that separated the Pacific Ocean from the Caribbean Sea. Although American officials thought they had reached an agreement with leaders of Colombia to develop the canal, Colombia refused to sign the final agreement. At the same time, people living in that region were pushing for their independence from Colombia. U.S. president Theodore Roosevelt decided to back the rebels, and in November 1903, the new nation of Panama declared its independence from Colombia. When Colombia prepared to fight the rebels, they found the U.S. Navy protecting Panama. Within a week, the United States

The Panama Canal might not have been built had the United States not chosen to back Panama in its bid for independence from Colombia.

and Panama had signed an agreement giving the United States the right to build and control the Panama Canal.

La Violencia

For the next few decades, life in Colombia was fairly peaceful. The Conservatives and the Liberals continued to oppose each other, however. Colombia was led by presidents from the Liberal Party from 1930 to 1942.

In 1948, Liberal presidential candidate Jorge Eliécer Gaitán was assassinated in Bogotá. Gaitán had been very popular among Colombia's lower class, and his assassin, Juan Roa Sierra, was beaten to death by a mob. Rumors about Gaitán's assassination swirled, but exactly who was behind

Roa was never proven. Most Liberals assumed Conservatives and their supporters had ordered the assassination, and battles between the groups broke out immediately.

The violence quickly spread throughout Bogotá and into the countryside. The first days of the violence, in and around Bogotá, were known as el Bogotazo. As the fighting spread, however, it became known simply as la violencia (the violence), and it showed no signs of stopping. Between 1948 and 1957, la violencia was responsible for the destruction of innumerable homes and villages and cost some 300,000 Colombian lives.

The National Front

In 1957, Liberals and Conservatives were finally able to come to an agreement to end the fighting. Beginning in 1958, a new government structure, called the National Front, went into effect. By this agreement both parties agreed that the presidency would alternate between the Liberals and Conservatives every four years. They also agreed to share power in legislative and local elections and collaborate on major decisions. This agreement allowed Colombia to break free from la violencia and achieve a brief period of relative peace.

Although it was difficult for the two sides to agree on major reforms or changes, the National Front was popular with many Colombians, because it reduced the warfare in the country. As years passed, however, the government's inability to address economic concerns caused some Colombians to lose faith in both the Conservatives and the Liberals. One such concern was a fall in the price of coffee in the early 1960s: Coffee was Colombia's main crop, and many people relied on it for their income.

Armed Rebels

As the economy declined, resistance to the government grew. In 1964, students who were inspired by the Communist government in Cuba formed the National Liberation Army (also called ELN for its Spanish initials). Two years later, the Revolutionary Armed Forces of Colombia (FARC) was formed by the Communist Party of Colombia, and in 1968, a third Communist group, the Popular Liberation Army (EPL), was created. In 1972, a fourth rebel group, called M-19 (Movement of April 19), was formed. M-19 was formed because its members believed their leader, a former Colombian dictator name Rojas Pinilla, had been cheated out of

Fighting guerilla warfare and terrorism, a police officer removes explosives planted on a flag by the Communist rebel group the ELN.

the presidency in the election of April 19, 1970. All four organizations were able to establish ties to Communist nations such as Cuba, the Soviet Union, and China, and all four engaged in acts of guerrilla warfare and terrorism. The growth of these four groups reflected the growing dissatisfaction with Colombia's two main political parties and a decreased confidence in the National Front.

Some of the resistance to the National Front government came from the fact that the Liberals and Conservatives did not allow other political parties to gain any power. Most of the resistance, however was a reaction to Colombia's declining economy. As the official economy faltered, illegal trade grew. By the early 1970s, growing numbers of Colombians turned to the illegal drug trade as a way to improve their own economic positions.

The Drug Trade

Drugs had been present in Colombia for a long time. Coca had been grown and chewed by native Colombians for centuries, and marijuana had been grown in Colombia for most of the 20th century. In the 1960s, increased demand for Colombian marijuana in the United States led to greater production and higher prices. This trend continued through the 1970s. By the end of the 1970s, Colombia was producing 70 percent of the foreign-grown marijuana in the United States. The economic impact on Colombia was significant: As many as 100,000 people were directly involved in growing, harvesting, and transporting the drug.

Beginning in the 1970s, cocaine, which is processed from the coca plant, followed the same pattern of development as marijuana had. Again, demand from the United States drove up prices and provided jobs and income for many Colombians. The difference between marijuana and cocaine was that cocaine brought in much more money. Soon it replaced marijuana as Colombia's most valuable export. The people in charge of the drug trade used their money to recruit and equip private armies to protect their industry.

By 1974, the peace that had been established by the National Front was gone. Instead, Colombia had an ineffective government, four Communist rebel groups, and several powerful and wealthy private armies

Women harvest coca leaves grown in a Colombian valley. Cocaine is processed from the leaves and has remained Colombia's most valuable export since the 1970s.

dedicated to preserving the drug trade. In the face of these problems, leaders of the Liberal and Conservative parties decided to abandon the National Front agreement and hold open elections. The Liberals won in 1974 and again in 1978, but the country was

rapidly becoming unmanageable. Each Communist group had its own guerrilla army and actively worked against the government. Although the EPL faded away, the other three rebel groups engaged in widespread murder, kidnappings, and attacks against government targets.

CHAPTER TWO

A Nation in Turmoil

By 1980, Colombia's drug organizations were as dangerous as the Communist rebel armies. The huge sums of money that were generated through the drug trade allowed drug lords to hire trained soldiers and build private armies, which were better armed than the militaries of many nations—including Colombia's. These armies terrorized anyone who opposed the drug trade: civilians, politicians, and Colombia's law enforcement agencies.

Colombia's Cartels

Eventually, huge sections of Colombia were under the control of the drug lords. One main location for the cocaine trade was the city of Medellín. There, Carlos Lehder, Pablo Escobar, and Jorge Luis Ochoa founded an organization called the Medellín Cartel (a cartel is an international business group). They ran Medellín and the surrounding countryside

Armed soldiers of the Revolutionary Armed Forces of Colombia (FARC) monitor a road near Florencia to prevent citizens from voting in a local election.

Panama's dictator Manuel Noriega was ousted by the United States government in 1990 and jailed for drug trafficking.

with absolute control. They rewarded those who worked with them and killed those who crossed them. Their main rival was a drug cartel in the city of Cali. Periodically, battles between the cartels would break out, killing Colombians who happened to be in the way.

The drug trade involved nations other than just Colombia and the United States. Much of the coca was grown in Bolivia and Peru, and Colombian drug armies controlled huge regions within those countries. They also developed regular air traffic between those nations and Colombia, where the coca was processed into cocaine. Other nations, including Panama, Nicaragua, Mexico, and several Caribbean islands, were involved in the transport of drugs from Colombia to the United States. Drug money helped support Panama's dictator, Manuel Noriega, who was deposed by the U.S. military in 1990 and jailed for drug crimes.

Rise of the Paramilitaries

Some members of Colombia's upper class began to form their own private security forces. Between the violence of the drug cartels and the kidnapping and attacks of the Communist groups, the wealthy felt they needed more protection than the Colombian police or army could provide. The largest of these groups, called paramilitaries, were the size of small armies. They most often fought against the Communist rebels, who wanted to take money and land away from the wealthy.

In many cases the paramilitaries made deals with the drug lords, helping protect the drug business against the rebels and the government in exchange for a share of the drug profits. Several of the groups eventually joined forces in a loosely structured organization called the United Self-Defense Groups of Colombia (AUC).

Increased Attacks

The government was unable to stop the violence. In 1985, M-19 broke a cease-fire with the government and launched an attack on the Palace of Justice in Bogotá. In the battle that followed between the military and the rebels, 115 people were killed, including 11 Supreme Court judges. The FARC had also signed the cease-fire and had developed a formal political party called the Patriotic Union (UP) to join the political process. Violence between the government and various groups of FARC guerrillas continued, however, and by 1987 the government declared the truce over. The ELN never signed the cease-fire, and although it was the smallest of the major rebel groups, it launched several successful attacks on government sites throughout the 1980s.

Among the most common targets were Colombia's coal and oil reserves. By 1986, Colombia was producing and exporting oil, which helped free the country from dependence on the price of coffee. Oil production gave the government a source of income that could rival the huge amounts of money brought in by drugs, allowing the government to

An injured man is evacuated from the Palace of Justice in Bogotá, Colombia, after M-19 rebels attacked the site in 1985.

spend more money on weapons and training for its soldiers. This made oil production sites especially attractive to all the enemies of the government.

By the late 1980s, most of Colombia was under the control of the paramilitaries, Communists, and cartels. The government maintained real control only in the major cities, and even there, kidnappings and murders happened regularly. As violence continued to increase throughout the country, the government began to use death squads to assassinate those suspected of working against the government.

The Cartels and the United States

The drug cartels were equally active. When the government sent Lehder to the United States to stand trial for drug offenses in 1987, the Medellín Cartel launched a series of attacks against government officials, seriously wounding a Colombian ambassador, kidnapping a son of a former president, and assassinating the attorney general. Lehder was convicted in U.S. courts and sent to prison. That same year, the Colombian

Supreme Court declared it illegal to extradite, or send Colombian citizens, to the United States for prosecution. Later in 1987, Colombia released Lehder's partner, Ochoa, from prison rather than sending him to the United States for trial. The American government strongly protested this.

Colombia's relations with the United States were mixed throughout the 1980s. The United States was a major economic partner, representing about a third of Colombia's foreign trade and offering Colombia financial assistance. At the same time, American leaders were very concerned about the flow of drugs. They began to tie economic aid to Colombia's fight against drugs, requiring the Colombian government to take active steps against the cartels.

A Tangled Web

For Colombia, challenging the drug cartels was more difficult than simply facing their armies and invading their strongholds. Some of the wealthiest people in Colombia secretly supported the cartels, in part because they were paid by the drug lords and in part because the cartels frequently fought against the Communists. The government death squads and paramilitaries, funded by drug money, often worked together against the rebels. It was also dangerous to run for political office against the drug lords. Three antidrug presidential candidates were assassinated before the 1990 election.

The cartel leaders realized that the Colombian government could not devote all its attention to them as long as the Communist rebels were active. To protect themselves, the cartels gave money and support to both the paramilitaries and the rebel groups. This meant that both the wealthy

PABLO ESCOBAR

Born in Medellín in 1949, Pablo Emilio Escobar Gaviria grew up stealing cars and selling drugs. In the 1970s, he became more involved in the drug trade, selling and using marijuana and later cocaine. Known for his brutality, Escobar was feared by many in Medellín.

Around 1980, Escobar joined Carlos Lehder and Jorge Luis Ochoa in forming what became known as the Medellín Cartel. This organization began transporting cocaine out of Colombia; most of it went to the United States. It had fleets of airplanes, ships, and trucks and completely controlled the region around Medellín; anyone who worked against the cartel was likely to be killed.

Escobar was particularly feared. There were many reports that he personally executed people who crossed him. He was also considered responsible for ordering the assassinations of political leaders, judges, and other officials who threatened the drug trade. Even his own partners feared him. In an interview on PBS's *Frontline* in October 2000, Ochoa explained, "You couldn't confront Pablo Escobar, because you knew what would happen: you would die. You couldn't confront him at all."

Throughout the 1980s, the United States increased pressure on Colombia's government to reign in the drug cartels. The only thing that Escobar feared was extradition to the United States, where his power might not protect him. In 1991, Escobar agreed to remain under house arrest, staying in a resort home that he had built. In 1992, though, fearing that he might be extradited, he fled.

Colombia created a special group called the Search Block to go after Escobar. Trained by U.S. Special Forces teams, the Search Block was authorized to kill Escobar if

SE BUSCA

PABLO EMILIO ESCOBAR GAVIRIA

SOLICITADO POR LA JUSTICIA

A QUIEN SUMINISTRE INFORMACION QUE PERMITA SU CAPTURA
EL GOBIERNO NACIONAL LE OFRECE COMO GRATIFICACION

$ 1.000'000.000.oo
MIL MILLONES DE PESOS

Described as ruthless, drug trafficker Pablo Escobar was one of the most feared leaders of the Medellín Cartel.

---

needed. At the same time, a group called Los Pepes, made up of Escobar's enemies, was also looking to kill him. On December 2, 1993, Search Block found him first. Escobar was killed in that raid, and the Medellín Cartel broke apart soon after.

and their most direct enemies profited from the illegal drugs. It also meant that the government could not isolate any one of their problems from the others: The cartels, Communists, and paramilitaries were all intertwined.

In 1989, the government managed to reduce its number of enemies by one. M-19 had been weakened since its 1985 attack on the Palace of Justice. All 35 members who participated in that attack were killed, and in 1987, one of its primary leaders was assassinated. In 1989, the government and M-19's remaining leadership negotiated peace. Although one small faction of M-19 remained active, the peace held, even when several former members were assassinated by the paramilitaries in the early 1990s.

Even after M-19 disbanded as a guerrilla force, however, the ELN and FARC remained active. In 1996, the National Congress of the ELN published a statement of its political goals. Among those goals was the idea most feared by the wealthy and the drug lords: "An agrarian [land] reform will take place with the property of the large landowners, drug traffickers and latifundistas (plantation owners) being distributed among the landless peasants."[3]

Challenging the Drug Lords

After M-19 was disbanded, the Colombian government decided to focus its primary attention on the drug cartels, despite the continued threat of FARC and ELN. The largest and most dangerous cartel was the Medellín Cartel, led by Escobar. Arrested in 1991, he was influential enough to arrange that he be only lightly guarded in a private home, from which he easily escaped. In 1993, an elite military team tracked Escobar down and killed him in a shootout. This led to the collapse of the Medellín

Medellín Cartel leader Pablo Escobar (on the ground) was killed by the Search Block in a December 1993 raid.

Cartel, which broke into several smaller organizations. Over the next several years, a series of arrests of Cali leaders limited that organization's operations as well. Then in 1997, the constitution was changed to again allow extradition of drug criminals to the United States.

Not everyone in Colombia's government strongly opposed the drug trade, though. Some of the connections between drugs and government in Colombia were highlighted in 1994. Ernesto Samper Pizano was elected president in that year, promising to bring the drug lords and Communist rebels under control. Soon, however, he was accused of accepting drug money. Opponents claimed that a significant amount of the money he used to run

Increased efforts to fight the drug cartel of Cali, Colombia, led to the government's seizure of 1,200 kilograms of cocaine packets in 2000.

for president came from drug traffickers. Although Samper was never convicted in court, many Colombians and international observers believed the charges. After that, no one trusted him to take on the drug lords. Nor did he have much more success against the Communists. His army suffered several defeats against the FARC guerrillas. Samper's term ended without any major success against any of the Colombian government's enemies.

A New Plan

In 1998, Conservative candidate Andres Pastrana Arango was elected president. With the support of U.S. president Bill Clinton, Pastrana launched his Plan Colombia in 1999. The goals of this plan were to achieve peace with the Communists and the paramilitaries, combat the drug trade, support human rights, and build Colombia's economy. The main target was the drug trade, because Pastrana believed that if he could limit the drug lords' profits, it would decrease funding for both the paramilitaries and the Communists, making them each easier to face. Also, the drug trade was of great concern to the United States.

In July 2000, the United States approved a $1.3 billion aid package, above the $300 million that had already been promised to Colombia. Most of this money was to train and equip the Colombian antidrug forces. The United States began taking a more direct role in some parts of the fight against drugs in Colombia. U.S. pilots flew crop-dusting aircraft that dropped herbicide on areas where drugs were grown. They also worked with the Colombian military to track and shoot down planes used to transport drugs. Those operations were suspended for two years, however, after an American missionary and her child were killed when their plane was shot down in 2001.

Pastrana also tried to establish peace with the FARC, which had become the largest rebel group. He granted them a safe zone in central Colombia—a huge area roughly the size of Switzerland. He hoped to convince the FARC to stop fighting and begin serious peace talks. Although there were some talks, the violence never really stopped. After a series of new attacks by FARC in 2002, Pastrana ordered his troops back into the safe zone.

Colombia's constitution does not allow a president to be reelected, so despite some success in his Plan Colombia, Pastrana was forced to step down when his term ended in 2002. The voters selected Alvaro Uribe, an independent candidate who was not a member of the Liberal or Conservative parties. Uribe promised to continue and even expand Plan Colombia, and he was strongly supported by U.S. president George W. Bush. The challenge of his job was apparent as bombs exploded around the presidential palace on his inauguration. Uribe survived, but the road to keep his promise of peace would be a long one.

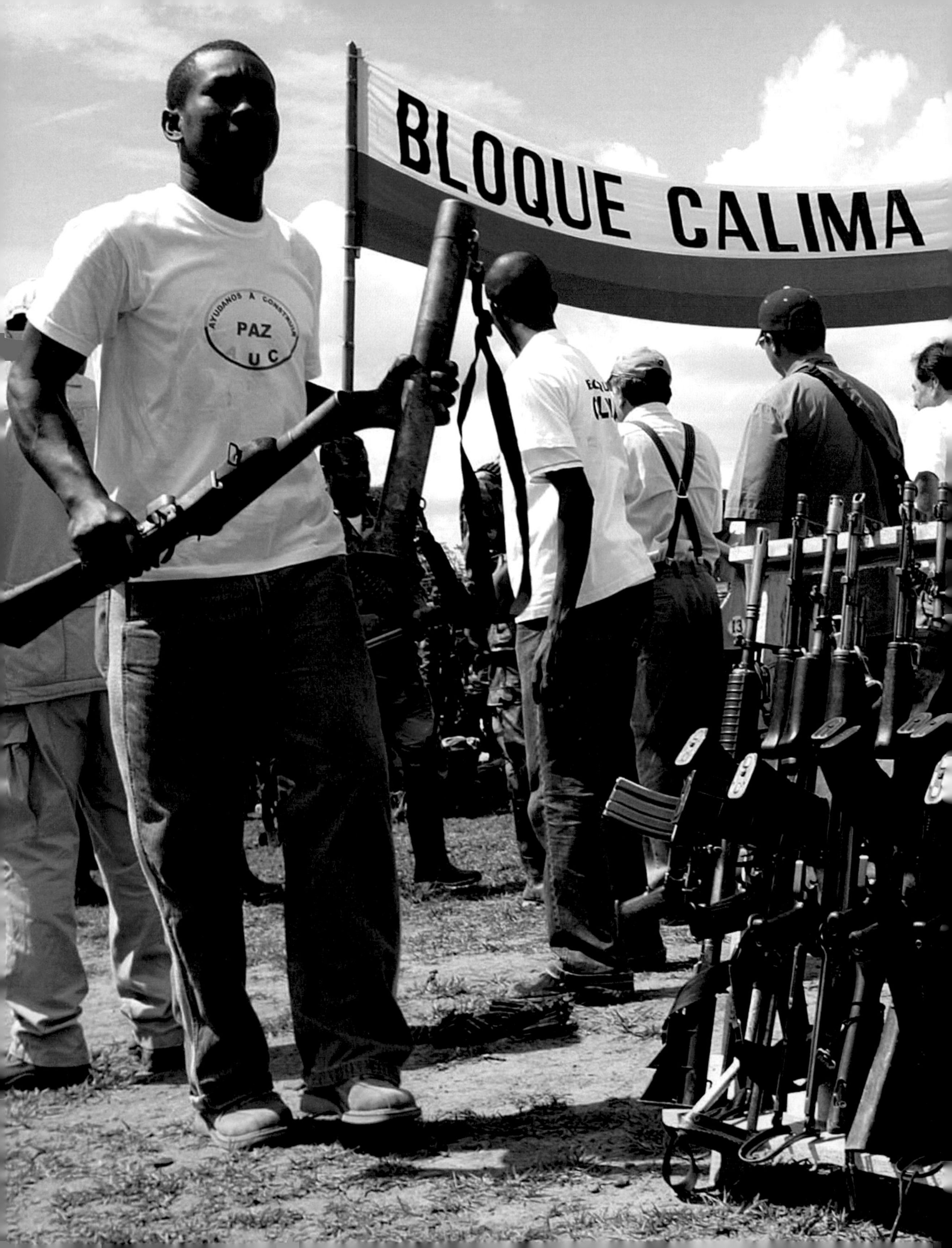
BLOQUE CALIMA
AYUDANOS A CONSTRUIR
PAZ

CHAPTER THREE

Colombia's Future

In his first two years in office, Uribe was able to decrease coca cultivation by 30 percent. This meant both destroying the coca plants and providing the local farmers with alternative crops to grow. Government officials had to convince farmers to grow these crops, giving up the huge profits they were making growing marijuana, coca, and, increasingly, opium poppies used to produce heroin. They also had to convince the farmers that the government could protect them from the drug lords and guerrillas who depended on the drug crops. In areas not under direct government control, many farmers did not trust the government's promises of safety, and Uribe had only limited success in those regions.

Expanding the Plan

To achieve peace, Uribe had to try to separate Colombia's three violent opposition groups. Plan Colombia had tried to address both the drug traffic and the FARC, with mixed success. Uribe turned his attention to the paramilitaries. Uribe and leaders of the AUC came to an agreement in

Over 3,000 members of the paramilitary group the AUC turned in their weapons to the Colombian government in December 2004.

With support from the U. S. government, the Colombian army has taken a stand against drug cartels by spraying herbicides on opium poppy fields, as this plane is doing.

2003. The group promised to disarm by the time Uribe's term expired in 2006. By December 2004, an estimated 3,000 of the 20,000 members of the AUC had disarmed.

Even disarming the AUC did not remove the conflict over the paramilitaries, however. One major question Colombia faced was what to do with their members. Uribe hoped to offer deals to any AUC members who voluntarily surrendered: In many cases, they would serve from three to ten years under house arrest. Many members of Colombia's congress, though, demanded real prison time and a return of the money and property the paramilitaries gained through their activities. That conflict remained unresolved through the middle of Uribe's presidency.

U.S. Concerns

Uribe's hope to offer deals to AUC leaders also met resistance from the United States. The FARC, ELN, and AUC have all been officially classified as terrorist organizations by the United States, and several of their leaders are wanted in America for crimes involving both drugs and attacks against U.S. citizens. U.S. ambassador to Colombia William Wood described the AUC as, "Criminals, narco-traffickers [drug runners], assassins and thieves."[4] Colombia cannot easily grant amnesty, or reduced sentences, to any members of these groups without damaging its relationship with the American government.

Even if Colombia's congress and the United States allow Uribe to offer amnesty to AUC members in exchange for peace, many drug leaders who have worked alongside the paramilitaries would try to claim the same generous deals. This would put them outside the reach of the United States or the Colombian government for their drug crimes. This could threaten the good relations between the two nations.

Signs of Progress

Because the paramilitaries have relied on drug money, Uribe had to slow down the drug trade if he hoped to contain them. He took on the drug lords even more directly than Pastrana or his predecessors had. In his first two years in office, Uribe extradited more than 170 people to the United States to stand trial for drug offenses. This included Gilberto Rodriguez Orejuela, one of the founders of the Cali Cartel. Colombia and the United States also worked with the nations of Peru and Bolivia to end coca cultivation in those nations, hoping to limit the reach of the cartels.

Despite signs of progress, violence is still common in Colombia. Here, police carry the body of a fellow officer through the rubble of a building attacked by FARC.

Neither the talks with the AUC nor the increased pressure on the drug lords seemed to have much immediate impact on the FARC. Although the ELN was relatively quiet throughout the early years of Uribe's administration, the FARC showed few signs of stopping its activity. The largest guerrilla group in the Western Hemisphere, with as many as 18,000 members, the FARC still controlled a huge region of the country and still engaged in regular acts of terror and violence.

In January 2004, the government arrested one of the FARC's leaders, Ricardo Palmera. He was captured in Ecuador and extradited to the United States in December. In February 2005, Colombian forces with U.S. support captured Omaira Rojas Cabrera, another major FARC leader. She also was extradited to the United States to stand trial for drug charges. Although these were the two highest-ranking FARC officials ever captured, there was little indication that their capture would slow the FARC's antigovernment activities.

In fact, in parts of Colombia, the citizens remain concerned with Uribe's peace negotiations with the AUC because the people see the para-military as the only protection against the FARC. As one woman in a rural province stated, "Nobody here trusts the police or the army to protect us. It's not that we like the paramilitaries, but we owe them some gratitude."[5] Another man in the same town explained, "People were used to (the paramilitaries), and they gave us good security. The people felt more com-fortable, because the guerrillas fear the paramilitaries more than they fear the police and the army."[6] It is the people in these rural areas, far from government protection, who have suffered the most in Colombia.

Innocent Victims

For most of the past century, the main victims of the violence have been the campesinos (rural villagers). Caught between the Conservatives, Liberals, Communists, cartels, and paramilitaries, the average Colombian citizen has been used regularly by each group, forced to serve whomever is in power nearby, and frequently killed—sometimes just for being in the wrong place at the wrong time. Susan Lee, a director of Amnesty

International, stated that this was still a grave concern in 2005: "The human rights and humanitarian crises in Colombia remain critical with civilians targeted by all sides in the conflict—soldiers, army-backed paramilitaries and the guerrilla(s)."[7]

Throughout most of the 1990s and into the 21st century, Colombia had the highest murder and kidnapping rates by population in the world. In 2000, Colombia averaged more than ten kidnappings a day. Although Uribe was able to decrease these numbers in his first years in office, Colombia is still considered one of the world's most dangerous nations. As a result, approximately 1 million Colombians have left the country since 1996.

Often, those caught up in the struggle are children. According to a 2005 report by the Human Rights Watch Organization, "more than 11,000 children fight in Colombia's armed conflict, one of the highest totals in the world. At least one of every four irregular combatants in Colombia is under 18 years of age."[8]

Most of the violence stems from the drug organizations, Communist rebels, and paramilitaries, but the government has been responsible for its share as well. Reports of attacks by the government death squads were reduced under Uribe's presidency, but the close connections between Colombia's military and the paramilitary continue to be of concern. Several of Colombia's military leaders have been accused of supporting the paramilitaries and allowing the paramilitary soldiers to conduct attacks and assassinations against their joint enemies. The government is also accused of making mass arrests and engaging in human rights abuses, including torture and imprisonment without trial.

A woman walks past a Colombian army tank in her indigenous community. Innocent villagers like her are often caught in the violence between the government and rebel groups.

Future Plans

It is expected that Uribe will expand Plan Colombia beyond its set expiration date in 2005. Bush traveled to Colombia in November 2004 to reaffirm his support for Uribe and the fight against drugs, rebels, and paramilitaries. Bush promised to continue the high level of U.S. financial support. He also asked Congress to increase the number of U.S. service-men available to serve in Colombia.

MAS
(DEATH TO KIDNAPPERS)

In Colombia, the Communist guerrilla armies, drug traffickers, and paramilitaries are all threats to stability, and they are frequently intertwined. One of the best examples of the connections between these groups is the organization called Muerte a Secuestadores (MAS), or "Death to Kidnappers."

The drug lords financed both the paramilitaries and the Communists, knowing that each helped keep the government from focusing on the drug traffic. In 1982, however, the M-19 guerrillas kidnapped the sister of Jorge Luis Ochoa, one of the founders of the Medellín Cartel. They hoped to gain more money from the cartel by holding her for ransom. Ochoa, with his partners Carlos Lehder and Pablo Escobar, founded MAS, hiring 2,300 soldiers to go after the guerrillas. Even after Ochoa's sister was released, the organization continued to operate.

MAS began to work alongside Colombia's paramilitaries, fighting against the guerrillas of M-19, the FARC, and the ELN. In many cases, the government was accused of turning suspected guerrillas over to MAS or similar groups, who frequently tortured and killed the suspects. Soon, MAS joined the other paramilitaries that came together under the umbrella of the AUC. Over the years, MAS was blamed for killing thousands of guerrillas and people accused of supporting the guerrillas. It also was one of many connections between the drug lords and the paramilitaries, funneling drug money to the AUC leaders and using the AUC connections to sell drugs.

At a 2001 Mother's Day ceremony in Bogota, a grieving mother holds up a picture of her kidnapped son.

A popular president, Alvaro Uribe visits with citizens of Puerto Inirida in a show of support after their town was besieged by FARC guerillas in March 2005.

By the spring of 2005, Uribe had become one of the most popular presidents in Colombia's history. His approval rating reached as high as 70 percent, largely because of his success in reducing the murder and kidnapping rates and because of his willingness to take on the rebels, drug lords, and paramilitaries as he pushes for peace. He also promised to give land confiscated from drug traffickers to people who owned no land. His popularity was so high that there was talk of changing the constitution to allow him to run for president again when his term ends in 2006.

Uribe's high approval rating and popularity depend on his ability to continue to make progress toward peace in Colombia. Few countries have as much potential for growth. Between oil and coal deposits, strong industry, and agriculture, Colombia could be a model for development. International corporations would love to invest in Colombia's growth, and the nation's close partnership with the United States could open many doors in business and politics.

Children held a candlelight vigil for peace in Bogotá in 2001, but Colombia still remains one of the most dangerous nations in the world today.

For now, however, few businesses and governments will entrust their people or resources to Colombia while terror and violence are still so common. If Uribe and Colombia can continue to break down the drug organizations, establish a lasting truce with the FARC and ELN, and disband the paramilitaries, a bright future awaits. Until then, Colombia will remain near the top of the list of the world's most dangerous nations.

Important Dates

1525	First permanent Spanish settlement established in Colombia
1717	Spanish create Viceroyalty of New Granada, with the capital at Bogotá
1810	Revolution against Spain begins in Colombia
1819	Spain defeated at Battle of Boyacá; Gran Colombia established
1830	Venezuela and Ecuador secede from Greater Colombia
1899–1902	War of a Thousand Days
1903	Panama breaks free from Colombia with U.S. support
1948	Liberal Jorge Eliécer Gaitán assassinated; el Bogotazo marks beginning of la violencia
1957–1958	La violencia ends after some 300,000 deaths; Liberal and Conservative parties agree on creation of National Front government
1964–1966	The ELN and FARC Communist guerrilla movements develop
1972	M-19 pro-Communist guerrilla army founded
1985	M-19 launches attack on Palace of Justice
1987	Medellín kingpin Carlos Lehder extradited to the United States; Colombian Supreme Court later voids extradition policy
1989–1990	Three presidential candidates assassinated; peace agreement reached with M-19
1993	Medellín's Pablo Escobar killed by government antidrug forces
1994	Ernesto Samper elected president, but accused of accepting drug money for his campaign
1998–1999	President Andres Pastrana (Conservative) launches Plan Colombia; grants safe zone to the FARC to promote peace talks
2000	United States approves $1.3 billion additional aid in support of Plan Colombia
2002	Pastrana ends the FARC safe zone; Alvaro Uribe becomes president; bombs strike presidential palace
2003	AUC leaders agree to begin disarming paramilitaries
2004–2005	Cali Cartel founder Gilberto Rodriguez Orejuela and FARC leaders Ricardo Palmera and Omaira Rojas Cabrera arrested and extradited to the United States

For More Information

BOOKS

Sara Cameron, *Out of War: True Stories from the Front Lines of the Children's Movement for Peace in Colombia.* New York: Scholastic, 2001.

Krzysztof Dydyniski, *Lonely Planet: Colombia.* Oakland: Lonely Planet, 2003.

Peg Lopata, *Colombia.* San Diego: Lucent Books, 2004.

Marion Morrison, *Colombia.* New York: Children's, 1999.

Mary M. Rodgers, *Colombia in Pictures.* Minneapolis: Lerner, 1987.

WEB SITES

National Memorial Institute for the Prevention of Terrorism (www.tkb.org/Country.jsp?countryCd=CO). Contains detailed information on both major and minor Colombian terrorist groups. Includes country statistics and reports on "Patterns of Global Terrorism" from the last 20 years.

Revolutionary Armed Forces of Colombia (www.farcep.org/pagina_ingles). English language page for the FARC.

U.S. State Department Background Notes: Colombia (www.state.gov/r/pa/ei/bgn/35754.htm). Detailed description of Colombian history, politics, trade, military, standard of living, and formal political relations with the United States.

The World Factbook: Colombia (www.cia.gov/cia/publications/factbook/geos.co.html). Contains country information and statistics on Colombia's population, economy, government, international relations, and other important categories, updated regularly.

Source Quotations

1. Human Rights Watch, "Human Rights Overview: Colombia," January 2004. http://hrw.org/english/docs/2004/01/21/colomb6978.htm.

2. United Nations Development Programme, "Biodiversity Conservation in the Chocó Biogeographic Region," May 1991–December 1999. www.gefweb.org/Outreach/outreach-publications/Project_factsheet/Colombia-biod-1-bd-undp-eng-ld.pdf.

3. National Congress of the ELN, "ELN's Political Agenda," July 1996, as reported by PBS Online News Hour. www.pbs.org/newshour/bb/latin_america/colombia/players_eln.html.

4. Quoted in "Lording It over Colombia," *Economist*, October 21, 2004.

5. Quoted in Kevin Sullivan, "Disarmament Holds Out Hope for Elusive Peace in Colombia," *Washington Post,* December 26, 2004.

6. Quoted in Sullivan "Disarmament Holds Out Hope for Elusive Peace in Colombia."

7. Quoted in Amnesty International, "International Community Must Demand Action on Human Rights," February 1, 2005.

8. Human Rights Watch, "Colombia: Armed Groups Send Children to War," February 22, 2005. http://hrw.org/english/docs/2005/02/22/columb10202.htm.

Index

About the Author

Chris Hughes holds a B.A. in history from Lafayette College and an M.A. in social studies education from Lehigh University. A history teacher and school administrator, Hughes teaches both U.S. and world history and has written several books on the American Civil War and on developing nations. Hughes currently lives and works at a boarding school in Chatham, Virginia, with his wife, Farida, and their children, Jordan and Leah.